Always be kind, even
when no one is watching.
love, Maritza

www.mascotbooks.com

Be Kind to Every Kind

For more information, please contact:
Mascot Books
620 Herndon Parkway #320
Herndon, VA 20170
info@mascotbooks.com

Library of Congress Control Number: 2018903778

CPSIA Code: BANG0518A
ISBN-13: 978-1-68401-930-4

Printed in the United States

BE KIND TO EVERY KIND

Extending Our Circle of Compassion to All Living Beings

Written and Illustrated by
Maritza Oliver

Introduction

Life isn't always fair. You are never too young to see injustice or to suffer from it. But even kids can do something about it—speak out in your classroom, name inequalities when you see them, or create after-school clubs where you discuss what you witness. March in the streets, sign a petition, write a letter or an editorial, volunteer in your community, or help an organization that you feel strongly about. Never be afraid to denounce what's not okay, but also remember that hatred is best countered with love and compassion. -Maritza Oliver

Some New Words

Bodily Autonomy: The right to rule over oneself

Cultural Mixing: The cultural variety that exists in the world or society

Dignity: The state of being worthy of respect

Discrimination: The unfair treatment of a group of people

Ethnicity: Cultural background

Inequality: An unfair situation where some people have more than others

Marginalize: Treat people as insignificant

Othering: Treating someone as different

Prejudice: To dislike someone without a good reason

Privilege: A special right that only some people have

Sentient: Able to perceive and feel

Speciesism: The belief that humans are superior to animals, leading to their exploitation

Status Quo: The way things currently are

Stereotype: A set idea about what people are like

A Note from the Author

As a mother, author, illustrator, and activist, my work reflects my life and the things that inspire me. My love for nature, animals, justice, equality, and desire to spread the vegan message are the driving force behind my creative process.

Vegan Children's Books' vision is represented through one promise:

"Love, Respect, and Compassion for All"

I hope my work inspires you to become an empowered voice for those who have been silenced.

I hope you enjoy reading and coloring each of these books as much as I enjoyed making them.

Thank you!

Other Books by Maritza Oliver

A Pig IS a Dog IS a Kid

Milk and Cookie a Little Spooky

Plant-Powered Buddies: My Coloring & Activity Books

Vegan Hearts Coloring Book

Our Planet, Our Home

We share this world with millions of other living creatures, including birds, fish, reptiles, amphibians, arthropods, and mammals (like humans). We are one big family, and since we all live on planet Earth, we are all earthlings.

Each life is precious, no matter who we are or who we love. Each earthling is unique, but we are much more alike than we are different. What is important is that we feel with our bodies and hearts and we want to live happily, safely, and in freedom. In this way, all beings are equal.

More than equals, we are individuals with rights! We have these rights regardless of race, color, creed, sex, or gender, whether we are old or young, big or small, rich or poor, abled or disabled, born here or anywhere else in the world.

The basic rights of food, water, and shelter belong to every person in the world, from birth until death, for the health and well-being of each one of us. We also have the rights to **bodily autonomy, dignity,** equality, and independence.

VOTE HERE

Despite the fact that everyone is entitled to their rights, some people are still treated unfairly, and their rights are ignored. This lack of fairness creates *inequality*, which is an injustice.

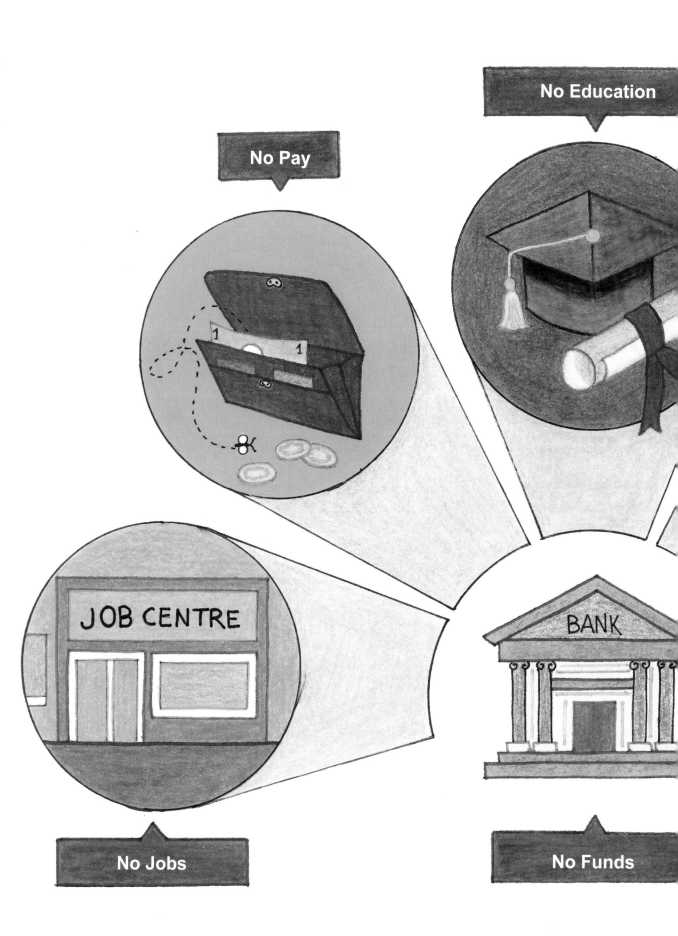

No Home

When society blocks people from their rights and benefits based on their social class, *ethnicity*, religion, gender, or ability, these people are considered to be *marginalized* or socially excluded.

On the other hand, when people have special rights and opportunities that are not able to be enjoyed by all or experience advantages over other people, these people are experiencing what it is called *privilege.*

Social Class

When those in power want to maintain the **status quo**, or want to move backwards to a less just society, they can marginalize people. This can lead to poverty, suffering, and sometimes even death.

When people don't have equal access to rights and opportunities due to discrimination, the result is called **social injustice.**

Social injustice is unfairness experienced by a group of people based on certain characteristics. Examples of such characteristics include race (racism), age (ageism), sex (sexism), gender (genderphobia), class (classism), and ability (ableism).

Social injustice comes in many forms and affects people all over the world!

Sometimes *prejudice* causes social injustice. Other times people in authority feel entitled to be cruel to someone just because they can. Not cool!

A Little Bit Different but Essentially the Same

At an early age we notice obvious differences between people. We tend to hang out with friends who are just like us. When we get to know people, even those who are different from us, they no longer feel so different.

When we see the similarities between ourselves and other people, it helps us resist forming *stereotypes*.

Noticing differences is natural, but it's important to avoid **othering** people, as if the group that we are part of (race, religion, ethnicity, gender, class, sexual orientation, etc.) is the "right" way to be human. This way of thinking—"us vs. them"—is harmful because it divides us.

Olá!

Namaste!

Sannu!

Diversity

Our society is diverse: it is made of different groups of people who unite to form many different types of communities. As different as we are, we are all born with open minds. We can all get along. People who get along with each other learn to work out their differences. So it's important to learn to live together in a peaceful way.

Szia!

Hello!

Salaam!

Nay Hoh!

Merhaba!

Jambo!

Hola!

Ciao!

This means respecting and understanding that each person is unique. The advantage of *cultural mixing* is that we have a far more exciting society. We get opportunities every day to learn about each other's cultures, support one another, and unite our various strengths in order to thrive!

Ni hau!

Ohayo!

Hallo!

Bonjour!

A More Inclusive Society

"I am Peruvian. I have personally experienced discrimination. People have treated me differently because of the colour of my skin, my ethnic background, my gender, my social class, my beliefs, and my physical appearance. I have felt hurt. I have felt anger. I have felt worried."

Empathy—the compassion that we discover by walking in another's shoes—comes through sharing our stories and experiences. When we or someone we like experiences discrimination, it's easy for us to care. If we care enough, we will increase our efforts to stop all discrimination and create a truly inclusive society. That's why it is so important to share our stories.

We can have a society that works for everyone by building great relationships and treating other people with kindness and respect. This will make us feel happier, more fulfilled, supported, and connected.

If we look through each other's eyes for an instant, if we acknowledge another's story; if we hear what they hear, see what they see, and feel what they feel… would we treat each other differently?

A More Just World

If we believe in equality, aligning our actions with our values will keep us true to ourselves. Racism, sexism, and other forms of discrimination are always wrong, and so is *speciesism.*

What a wonderful world we could create if we extended our circle of compassion to all beings, including animals! Both human and non-human animals are *sentient*—they feel with their hearts and bodies, no matter if they were born with fur, feathers, fins, or human skin. Every sentient being deserves rights.

A more peaceful world is possible. But it's up to all of us to find ways to create more empathy and understanding, to learn to live in harmony with each other, and not only to promote tolerance, but also promote true acceptance of a world that is good for animals, good for you, and good for me.

#BeKindtoEveryKind

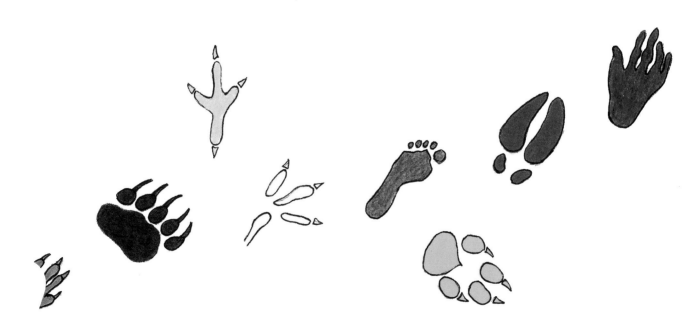